DATE DUE	

Trudi Strain Trueit

Octopuses, Squids, and Cuttlefish

Franklin Watts - A Division of Scholastic Inc.
New York • Toronto • London • Auckland • Sydney
Mexico City • New Delhi • Hong Kong
Danbury, Connecticut

For my sister Lori, a gentle friend to octopuses.
Special thanks to Roland C. Anderson and the Seattle Aquarium

Photographs © 2002: Animals Animals: 37 (Miriam Agron), 6, 29 (Bob Cranston), 27 (Steve Earley), cover, 5 top right (Bruce Watkins), 40 (Clay Wiseman); BBC Natural History Unit: 1 (Georgette Douwma), 7 (Jeff Rotman); Corbis Images/Reuters NewMedia Inc.: 33; Monterey Bay Aquarium Research Institute: 35 (Kim Reisenbichler), 23 (Dave Wrobel); Natural Visions/Peter David: 25, 31; Photo Researchers, NY: 12, 13 (David Hall), 41 (Geo. Lower), 42 (Copr. F. Stuart Westmorland); Visuals Unlimited: 5 bottom right (David S. Addison), 5 top left (Dave B. Fleetham), 19 (Alex Kerstitch), 16, 17 (Edward G. Lines), 15 (Ken Lucas), 21 (Steven N. Norvich), 39 (Science), 5 bottom left (David J. Wrobel).

Illustrations by Pedro Julio Gonzalez, Steve Savage, and A. Natacha Pimentel C.

The photograph on the cover shows a red octopus. The photograph on the title page shows a giant male cuttlefish.

Library of Congress Cataloging-in-Publication Data

Trueit, Trudi.
Octopuses, squids, and cuttlefish / by Trudi Strain Trueit; [Pedro Julio Gonzalez, Steve Savage, and A. Natacha Pimentel C., illustrators].
        p. cm. – (Animals in order)
    Includes bibliographical references and index.
    Summary: Describes the traits and classification of the aquatic mammals called coleoids, a subgroup of the cephalopods, with an emphasis on different kinds of octopuses, squids, and cuttlefish.
    ISBN 0-531-11930-0 (lib. bdg.)   0-531-16377-6 (pbk.)
    1. Cephalopoda—Juvenile literature. [1. Octopus 2. Squids 3. Cuttlefish 4. Cephalopoda.] I. Gonzalez, Pedro Julio, ill. II. Savage, Steve, ill. III. Pimentel C., A. Natacha, ill.
IV. Title. V. Series.
QL430.2.T78 2002
594'.56—dc21   2001005366

Contents

Are These Animals Related?

Have you ever come eye to eye with an octopus? You probably haven't in the ocean, but maybe you've seen one in an aquarium. You may have watched the rusty-red arms of a giant Pacific octopus dance around its soft, jellylike body. Perhaps a horizontal pupil seemed just as curious about you as you were about it. Octopuses are among the world's smartest *invertebrates*, or animals without backbones. They make up one group, or *order*, that belongs to a larger *subclass* of animals called *Coleoidea* (Coe-lee-oy-dee-uh).

For 500 million years, coleoids have lived on Earth. They were alive before dinosaurs and even fish had evolved. Long ago, these sea creatures had hard, outer shells. Today, what remains of these shells are usually inside their bodies. Some coleoids have lost their shells altogether.

Most coleoids have a well-developed head, featuring two large eyes that can see almost as well as you can. The head is connected to a muscular, saclike body called a *mantle*. All coleoids have eight arms that are attached to the head. Some also have two tentacles and a pair of fins.

Only three of the four animals on the next page are coleoids. Can you guess which one is not? Turn the page to see if you are right.

4

Nautilus

Market squid

Cuttlefish

Common octopus

Traits of Coleoids: Magicians of the Sea

If you chose the chambered nautilus, you are correct! Although the nautilus is related to coleoids, it lives inside a hard shell and has more than ninety tentacles.

A squid has a smaller shell, called a *pen*, within its body. It is made of *chitin* (KY-tin), which contains a material that makes it very hard. The calcium skeleton of a cuttlefish is called a *cuttlebone*. Unlike its relatives, most octopuses do not have shells.

The eight arms of coleoids have rows of suckers and sometimes hooks on the undersides. Squids and cuttlefish also have pairs of tentacles to help them catch *prey*, or food. Octopuses do not have tentacles. They use their arms and bodies to trap prey.

Coleoids eat with a parrotlike beak made of chitin. Inside the beak is a *radula*, which is a hard tongue covered with tiny, sharp teeth. Since coleoids have no bones, they can squeeze into any space that is large enough for their beaks to fit through.

These sea animals are experts at hiding from *predators*,

The beak of a coleoid is made of chitin.

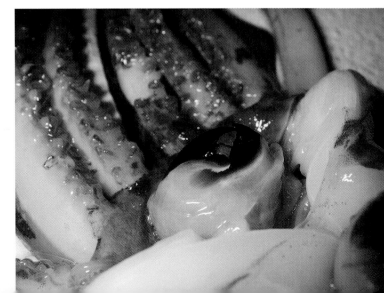

A coleoid may squirt ink into the water when it is frightened.

animals that hunt them for food. They can change color in less than one second—faster than any animal on Earth. Special color cells underneath the skin called *chromatophores* shrink into small dots to make the animal appear lighter, or grow larger to make the animal appear darker. This *camouflage* helps them blend in with their surroundings so they can catch prey and hide from predators.

When threatened, coleoids will squirt a dark ink cloud into the water, change color, and speed away. They can swim very quickly because they are jet propelled. Coleoids take water into their bodies, and then push it out at high pressure through *siphons*, the funnel on the side of a coleoid's mantel. The energetic squid uses jet propulsion to swim in the open ocean, while the slower, timid octopus uses it only to escape from predators.

Coleoids come in all shapes and sizes, from the inch-long pygmy octopus to the 60-foot- (18-m) long giant squid. Their average life spans vary from a few months to three years. Coleoids eat fishes, crabs, clams, oysters, mussels, shrimp, scallops, and sometimes other coleoids.

The Order of Living Things

A tiger has more in common with a house cat than with a daisy. A grasshopper is more like a butterfly than a jellyfish. Scientists arrange living things into groups based on how they look and how they act. A tiger and a house cat belong to the same group, but a daisy belongs to a different group.

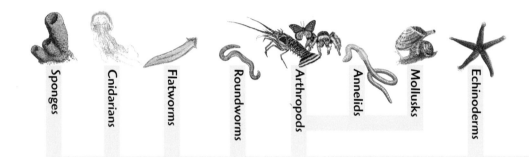

Sponges   Cnidarians   Flatworms   Roundworms   Arthropods   Annelids   Mollusks   Echinoderms

Animals

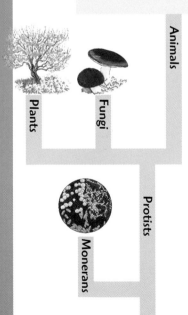

Plants   Fungi

Monerans

Protists

All living things can be placed in one of five groups called *kingdoms*: the plant kingdom, the animal kingdom, the fungus kingdom, the moneran kingdom, or the protist kingdom. You can probably name many of the creatures in the plant and animal kingdoms. The fungus kingdom includes mushrooms, yeasts, and molds. The moneran and protist kingdoms contain thousands of living things that are too small to see without a microscope.

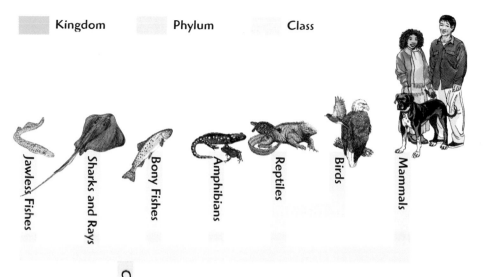

Kingdom   Phylum   Class

Jawless Fishes
Sharks and Rays
Bony Fishes
Amphibians
Reptiles
Birds
Mammals

Chordates

Because there are millions and millions of living things on Earth, some of the members of one kingdom may not seem all that similar. The animal kingdom includes creatures as different as tarantulas and trout, jellyfish and jaguars, salamanders and sparrows, elephants and earthworms.

To show that an elephant is more like a jaguar than an earthworm, scientists further separate the creatures in each kingdom into more specific groups. The animal kingdom can be divided into nine phyla. Humans belong to the chordate phylum. Almost all chordates have backbones.

Each phylum can be subdivided into many classes. Humans, mice, and elephants all belong to the mammal class. Each class can be further divided into orders; orders into families, families into genera, and genera into species. All the members of a species are very similar.

9

How Coleoidea Fit In

Coleoidea belong to the animal kingdom. They have more in common with spiders and starfish than they do with mushrooms and maple trees. Coleoids are part of the *mollusk* phylum. Mollusk comes from the Latin word *mollo,* which means "soft-bodied." Mollusks are invertebrates that have hard shells, or had them at an earlier evolutionary stage. Can you think of some other mollusks? Clams, scallops, oysters, snails, and even garden slugs are part of the mollusk phylum.

Mollusks can be divided into seven classes of living animals. The gastropods are one of these classes, and include snails and slugs. Oysters, clams, and scallops belong to the bivalves—animals with two shells that are connected by hinges.

Over millions of years, the shells of some mollusks changed shape, were covered by muscle tissue, or were lost completely. Octopuses, squids, cuttlefish, and nautiluses are members of the class *Cephalopoda.* The word cephalopod means "head-foot." It refers to how the arms and tentacles of the animal grow directly from its head.

Cephalopods live in water. They were once the main life form in the oceans, but today, less than one thousand species remain. They are found in every ocean in the world. Octopuses, squids, and cuttlefish are the three orders that make up the subclass Coleoidea (the nautilus has its own separate subclass, Nautiloidea). Scientists believe that most coleoids once had outer shells like the nautilus, but lost or covered them with body tissue millions of years ago.

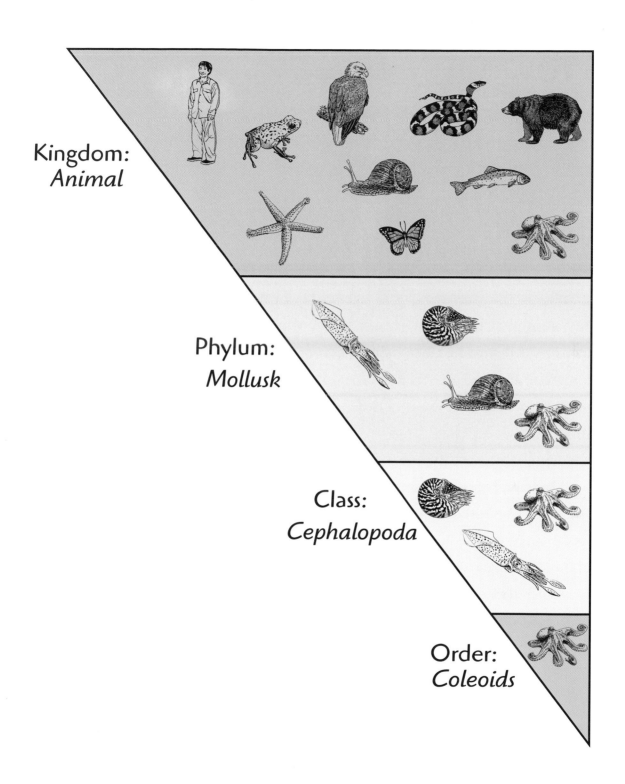

Kingdom:
Animal

Phylum:
Mollusk

Class:
Cephalopoda

Order:
Coleoids

Octopuses

FAMILY: Octopodidae

COMMON EXAMPLE: Common octopus

GENUS AND SPECIES: *Octopus vulgaris*

SIZE: to 3 feet (1 m)

LOCATION: Warm to temperate oceans
throughout the world

A common octopus hovers just above the ocean floor, dipping its arms into nooks and cracks. Each dotted, sandy-brown arm has two hundred powerful suckers. Each sucker has ten thousand *chemoreceptors* on it. These sensory organs can touch, smell, and even taste. Imagine having 16 million taste buds covering your arms to your fingertips!

The octopus spots a crab scrambling over a rock. It spreads the webbing between its arms out and stretches until it looks like a large umbrella. It then parachutes down on top of the crab and wraps it in its arms. There is nothing the crab can do. It would take 40 pounds (18 kg) of force to pry off the suckers of the 3-pound (1.4-kg) octopus. With one bite of its beak, the octopus poisons its prey. An octopus's beak is located under the mantle, at the central spot where the arms meet. After drilling a hole in the shell with its radula, the octopus injects a protein into the crab. This softens the meat so it can be sucked out.

Octopuses

FAMILY: Octopodidae
COMMON EXAMPLE: Pacific red octopus
GENUS AND SPECIES: *Octopus rubescens*
SIZE: to 12 inches (30 cm)
LOCATION: Pacific Ocean, from Alaska to
   Mexico

Two red octopuses are flashing colors at each other. It is a signal that they are ready to mate. The male uses the spoon-shaped tip at the end of one of its arms, called a *ligula*, to transfer packets of sperm into the female's mantle. The packets, called *spermatophores,* will fertilize her eggs.

Most octopuses live alone in a *den*, a lair they create under rocks, ledges, or piles of debris. Like many red octopuses, this female prefers to make her home in a soda bottle. Because she has no bones, she can easily slide into her small den. She attaches strings of eggs to the inside of the bottle. For the next four months she stands guard, spraying water over her five thousand eggs to clean them and give them oxygen. During this time, the female will not eat or leave her den.

As her offspring begin to hatch, she is already dying of starvation. A newborn red octopus is about the size of a pea. The thousands of tiny octopuses are no match for the sea stars, crabs, and fish that wait to eat them. Only a few of the babies will make it to adulthood.

Octopuses

FAMILY: Octopodidae
COMMON EXAMPLE: Giant Pacific octopus
GENUS AND SPECIES: *Enteroctopus dofleini*
SIZE: 8 to 25 feet (2 to 7 m)
LOCATION: Northern Pacific Ocean, from Japan to the United States

A giant Pacific octopus is being trailed by a hungry sea lion. Although it is the largest known octopus in the world, the giant is actually a shy animal. It would rather turn white, spray ink into the water, and jet away than fight the sea lion. Unfortunately, the giant octopus has many skilled predators, including moray eels, porpoises, and sharks.

Like most octopuses, the giant Pacific octopus tires easily. Octopuses have three hearts inside their mantles, but their blue, copper-based blood doesn't carry oxygen as well as does a human's iron-rich, red blood. Since the giant cannot outlast a predator in a chase, it must out-think the predator. If the sea lion attacks, the octopus has more than one trick up its sleeve, or rather, its arm. It can let the predator bite off an arm while it escapes. Many octopuses can regrow a damaged arm, but the new arm is often shorter than the original.

With a life span of about three years, the giant octopus is one of the longest-living coleoids. A 50-pound (23-kg) giant octopus eats about 2 pounds (1 kg) of food and gains 2 percent of its body weight each day. The largest giant Pacific octopus ever caught weighed 600 pounds (276 kg) and measured 31 feet (9 m) across.

Octopuses

FAMILY: Octopodidae

COMMON EXAMPLE: Greater blue-ringed octopus

GENUS AND SPECIES: *Hapalochlaena lunulata*

SIZE: to 3 inches (7 cm)

LOCATION: Western Pacific Ocean, near Indonesia, the Philippines, and Australia

You dip your toe into the cool waters of a tide pool, when suddenly you spy a brownish-gold octopus with bright blue rings. You reach down to touch the blue rings that appear to be three-dimensional. But beware! This beautiful octopus, which is no bigger than a tennis ball, carries one of the most deadly poisons in the world. A blue-ringed octopus weighing just 1 ounce (30 g) has enough venom in it to paralyze ten adults!

The blue-ringed octopus is timid and prefers to camouflage itself in a cloak of brown. Only when it feels that it is in danger will it flash its rings as a warning. Since the bite of this octopus is painless, a victim may not know that he or she has been poisoned. Several people have died from handling some species of blue-ringed octopuses.

The female of this species does not string her eggs in a den. Instead, she carries them with her. Scientists believe there are at least ten different species of blue-ringed octopuses—all of which are considered to be dangerous.

Octopuses

FAMILY: Octopodidae

COMMON EXAMPLE: Mimic octopus

GENUS AND SPECIES: (not yet classified)

SIZE: to 12 inches (30 cm)

LOCATION: Western Pacific Ocean, near Australia and Indonesia; Indian Ocean; and the Red Sea

A lionfish juts out its poison-tipped spines to warn predators that it is dangerous. But wait! It isn't a deadly lionfish at all. It is a reddish-brown and white-striped mimic octopus. It has spread its arms to make them look like spines. It is only pretending to be the dangerous lionfish.

The mimic octopus has earned its name because it is an expert at copying other animals. It can change color, texture, and form to resemble shrimp, stingrays, eels, crabs, and even sea horses. It can move like these animals, too. Flattening its body, it can pulsate through the water the way flounders do. Or it might stretch out two legs and wriggle along the ocean floor like a poisonous sea snake.

Scientists aren't sure how mimic octopuses learned to imitate other animals or why they do it, although it is probably a way to frighten off predators. Of course, this doesn't explain why the mimic pretends to be the peaceful, harmless seahorse. While most octopuses hunt at night, the mimic octopus hunts during the day.

Octopuses

FAMILY: Opisthoteuthidae

COMMON EXAMPLE: Dumbo octopus

GENUS AND SPECIES: *Grimpoteuthis* (species not yet classified)

SIZE: to 8 inches (20 cm)

LOCATION: Pacific Ocean (may also be in other oceans); deep sea to 1,300 feet (400 m)

The dumbo octopus drifts like an orange bell in the ocean current. This unusual creature gets its name from the two fins on its head, which make it look like a cartoon elephant. The dumbo is one of the few octopuses to have an internal shell, which helps support it as it floats in the water.

This species swims by moving its fins, pulsating its webbed arms, jet propulsion, or by doing all three at once. Along with suckers, thin sensory organs called *cirri* line the bottom of its arms. Scientists believe the cirri beat against the water to push worms, snails, and other food toward the dumbo's mouth. Since these deep-sea octopuses stay near the ocean floor, very few people have seen them. Much of the dumbos' eating, mating, and living habits remain a mystery. Robotic submarines have given scientists their first photographs of these mysterious octopuses.

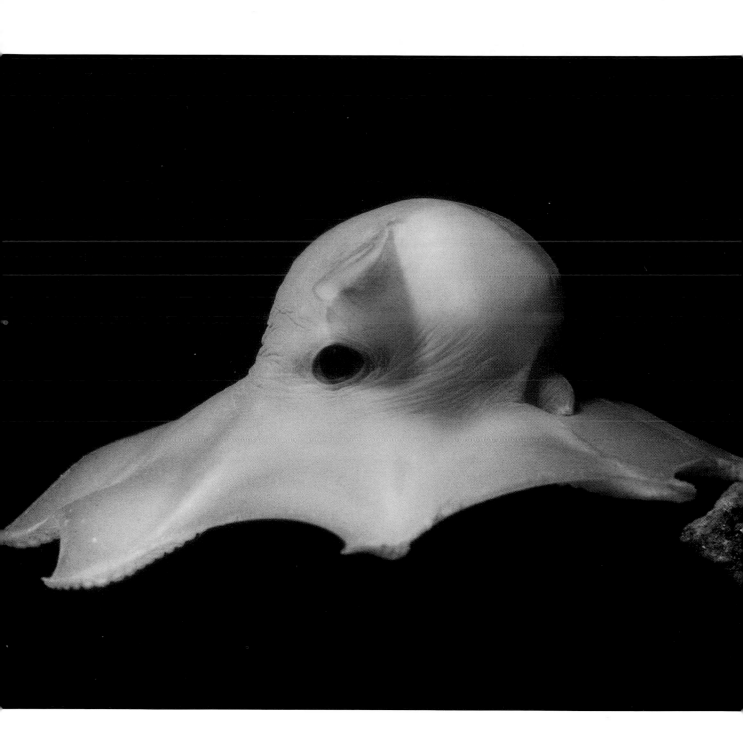

Argonauts

FAMILY: Argonautoidea

COMMON NAME: Greater argonaut

GENUS AND SPECIES: *Argonauta argo*

SIZE: females to 18 inches (45 cm), males to 0.8 inches (2 cm)

LOCATION: Tropical and subtropical waters throughout the world

At first glance, it would seem that the argonaut, with its ridged shell, has more in common with a nautilus than with a coleoid. In fact, argonauts are sometimes called "paper nautiluses." But it is an octopus. It has two eyes, eight arms, an ink sac, and uses jet propulsion and camouflage.

A baby female argonaut looks very much like a normal octopus, but two of her arms have special webbing. When she is young, she uses this webbing to secrete calcium and create her outer shell. She uses two of her other arms to hold the thin, brittle covering in place. She can leave this shell behind if necessary. Scientists believe that if the delicate shell is damaged, the argonaut can repair it. The female will use her shell as a case, or sac, for her eggs. Male argonauts have no shells and are dwarves, much smaller in size than the females.

Argonauts swim freely in the open sea. They eat jellyfish, shrimp, and crabs.

Squids

FAMILY: Loliginidae

COMMON EXAMPLE: California market squid

GENUS AND SPECIES: *Loligo opalescens*

SIZE: to 8 inches (19 cm)

LOCATION: Eastern Pacific Ocean, from Alaska to Mexico

A frenzy of bodies torpedoes through the water. Thousands of small, silvery squid are waving ribbons of colors at each other with their chromatophores. While octopuses usually creep slowly along the ocean floor, most squids are bundles of energy. Jet propulsion and two fins allow the market squid to cruise at about 2 miles (3 km) per hour, with short bursts of up to 10 miles (16 km) per hour.

Each autumn, schools of California market squid travel from the deep seas into shallow waters to mate. They live only a year and breed for just one season. After mating, a female wraps her eggs in a white, jellylike case and attaches it to the ocean floor. Off the California coast during mating season, the bottom of the sea is a blanket of white egg cases. After the eggs are laid, the mating pair will die. It takes about a month for the babies to hatch. Many of the tiny newborns will become prey. Others will be caught by local fishermen as they grow. Squid is a popular, tasty food for humans and is eaten around the world.

Squids

FAMILY: Ommastrephidae
COMMON EXAMPLE: Humboldt or jumbo
   flying squid
GENUS AND SPECIES: *Dosidicus gigas*
SIZE: to 13 feet (4 m)
LOCATION: Eastern Pacific Ocean, from
   California to the tip of South America

Humboldts, or jumbo flying squids, are fast, muscular predators that hunt in packs. The Humboldt's bullet-shaped body has two large fins, eyes the size of softballs, and a powerful siphon. It has a beak that is so strong that it can bite the oar of a boat in two. Two tentacles stretch out and then snap back like rubber bands. Horny hooks on the tentacles help the squid hold on to its prey. Humboldts have attacked scuba divers, mistaking them for food. A pack of squids may wrap their tentacles around a human, sinking their sharp hooks into the skin.

The Humboldt is part of the family of "flying squids." It can reach speeds of about 10 miles (16 km) per hour under water. It can jet so quickly it actually launches itself out of the sea and into the air. Some species in this family, such as the neon flying squid, can glide 60 feet (18 m) through the air. Many sailors have been surprised to see squids rocketing out of the ocean and landing on their boat decks.

Squids

FAMILY: Histioteuthidae
COMMON EXAMPLE: Cockeyed squid
GENUS AND SPECIES: *Histioteuthis heteropsis*
SIZE: to 8 inches (20 cm)
LOCATION: Indian and Pacific Ocean;
  deep-sea to 2,000 feet (800 m)

The cockeyed squid glides through the sea with its tiny white lights glittering across its body. In the deepest part of the ocean where the sun does not shine, animals like the cockeyed squid are *bioluminescent* and create their own light.

Rows of light-producing organs, called *photophores*, dot the squid's arms, head, and mantle. They make it look a little like a floating strawberry. The photophores light up when two chemicals in the skin react together. Bioluminescent squids can glow in color combinations of red, blue, green, yellow, and white. The flashing colors are a way of communicating, attracting prey, and confusing predators. Some bioluminescent squids can even release glowing ink clouds.

The cockeyed squid is named for its two very different eyes. One eye is small, blue, and sunken, while the other is twice its size, yellow, and bulges out of the head. Scientists think that one eye might see better in shallow water and the other might see better in deep water.

Squids

FAMILY: Architeuthidae

COMMON EXAMPLE: Giant squid

GENUS AND SPECIES: *Architeuthis dux*

SIZE: to 60 feet (18 m)

LOCATION: Oceans throughout the world;
deep sea to 3,000 feet (900 m)

Bigger than most dinosaurs and whales, the giant squid is the largest invertebrate Earth has ever known. Its eyes are the size of car hubcaps. Its two tentacles can measure 30 feet (9 m) in length. Despite its size, no one has ever seen a giant squid alive in the sea. Most of what we know about it comes from pieces of the giant found in the stomachs of sperm whales (its only known predator) or dead squids caught in fishing nets or washed ashore.

Legends, such as Jules Verne's *Twenty-Thousand Leagues Under the Sea*, paint the giant squid as a violent beast. But scientists say that this is an unlikely portrait. Giant squids, with their small fins and spongy bodies, are probably slow swimmers. Their soft muscles probably prevent them from being aggressive hunters. Scientists believe that giant squids may be smarter than octopuses, but they can't be sure because no one has ever been able to study or observe these large animals.

What do giant squid eat? How long do they live? How many species are out there? No one knows.

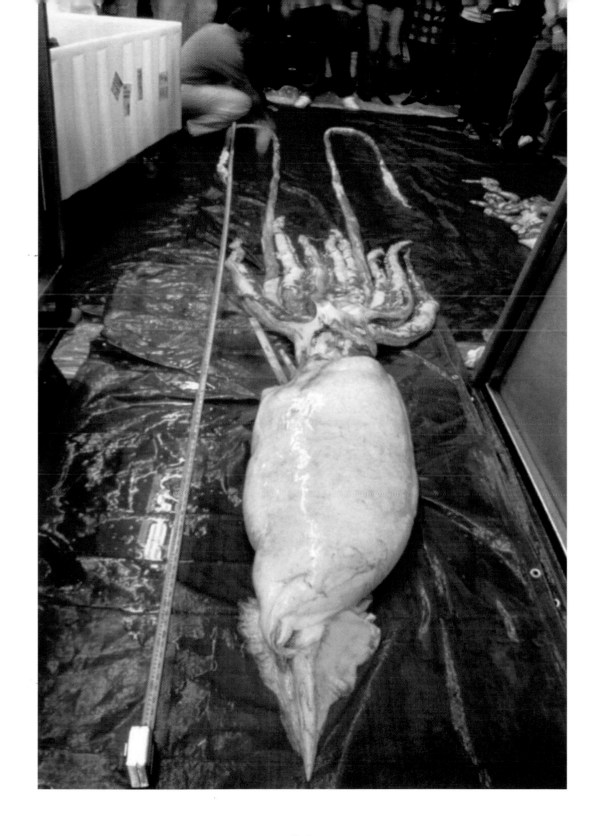

Squids

FAMILY: Vampyroteuthidae

COMMON EXAMPLE: Vampire squid

GENUS AND SPECIES: *Vampyroteuthis infernalis*

SIZE: to 1 foot (30 cm)

LOCATION: Temperate and tropical waters throughout the world; deep sea to 4,000 feet (1,200 m)

In the depths of the ocean drifts a purplish-red creature with giant blue eyes. It drags two strange, wispy fibers behind it. The vampire squid isn't really a squid and it isn't an octopus, though it shares some features with both. Some scientists believe that this wonder of the sea may be the species that links the two.

The vampire squid's large, winglike fins help it move through the water. It has eight webbed arms, each with one row of suckers. Instead of tentacles, the squid has two lacy filaments that look like sheer curtains. It can tuck them into pockets between its arms. Scientists think the filaments may be used like a net to haul in prey.

The vampire squid was named for the black cloak that appears when it pulls its webbed arms over its head for protection. Bioluminescent lights near the fins and along the arms can be flickered on and off to confuse predators. The vampire squid does not have ink, but it can shoot out a luminescent cloud that may glow for up to 10 minutes.

Cuttlefish

FAMILY: Sepiidae
COMMON EXAMPLE: European common cuttlefish
GENUS AND SPECIES: *Sepia officinalis*
SIZE: to 18 inches (45 cm)
LOCATION: Eastern Atlantic Ocean, Mediterranean Sea, North Sea, and the Baltic Sea

Zebra stripes ripple across the skin of the male European common cuttlefish. Cuttlefish come in more color combinations than any other animal on Earth. They use at least fifty colors and patterns to communicate, lure prey, and camouflage themselves.

A male may flash mating colors to a female on one side of his body while his other side sends a warning glow to a competing male. A male and female cuttlefish mate face to face. They weave their tentacles together and the male passes his spermatophores to his mate. The female attaches her black eggs to seaweed, rocks, or debris. She does not watch over the eggs. Soon after the cluster of eggs is laid, the mating pair will die. A month later, the young cuttlefish are born. They spend the first part of their lives hidden in the sand on the ocean floor so predators will not eat them.

People used to hunt the common cuttlefish for its ink, known as sepia. The dark-brown liquid was once widely used for writing and drawing.

Cuttlefish

FAMILY: Sepiidae
COMMON EXAMPLE: Giant cuttlefish
GENUS AND SPECIES: *Sepia apama*
SIZE: to 3 feet (1 m)
LOCATION: Pacific Ocean, near Australia

A giant cuttlefish lurks in the seaweed, its body perfectly matching the deep greens of the grasses. Papery fins run the length of its mantle, allowing it to move forward, backward, or side to side. To sink and rise, it fills and empties its skeletal cuttlebone with gas.

Suddenly, the cuttlefish shoots out its two tentacles like whips and grabs a passing shrimp. The tentacles, which it usually keeps tucked into pouches underneath its body, can stretch nearly 2 feet (0.6 m). Since it has no hooks, a cuttlefish will often use the sea floor and its own body to trap fish, crabs, and shrimp. It may also bury itself in the sand to wait for prey or to avoid predators.

The colorful giant is the largest cuttlefish in the world. Each May, tourists flock to southern Australia to see the thousands of cuttlefish that come to the shallow waters to breed. Cuttlefish are curious and not usually a threat to people, but they have been known to bite divers who have gotten too close to them.

39

Clever Kaleidoscopes

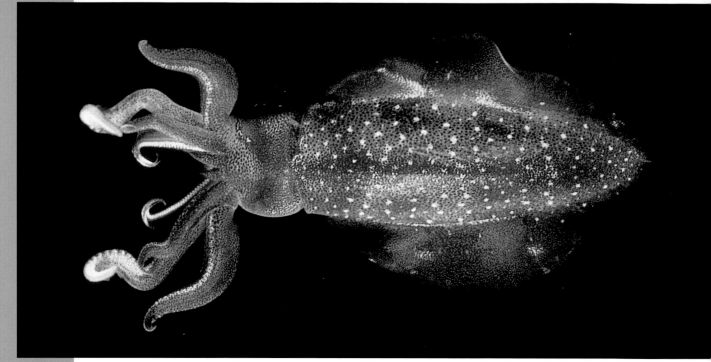

This Atlantic oval squid has glowing spots.

From the dazzling lights of a deep-sea squid to the red flush of an angry octopus, coleoids write their feelings across their bodies in vivid colors. An adult coleoid has millions of chromatophores it uses for communication and camouflage. A frightened octopus may turn white, while a happy one is a patchwork quilt of browns. Mating rituals include flashing stripes, dots, and blotches. Skin texture can shift from marble smooth to pebbly bumps in seconds, matching the sea floor, a rock, or whatever surroundings the animal wants to blend with. Octopuses will often try to mimic stones. Squids can appear to be drifting seaweed. Some types of cuttlefish sport two black dots, or "eyes," on their backs as they pretend to be the head of a large animal. Even baby octopuses and cuttlefish have plenty of chromatophores to begin changing colors from the moment they are born. Coleoids use their many different colors, patterns, and textures to express several thousand meanings that only they are able to fully understand.

Scientists are discovering that the minds of coleoids may be just as complex as their wardrobes. It's believed that most octopuses have about the same intelligence as mice. The common octopus (*Octopus vulgaris*) shows signs of being almost as smart as a cat.

In laboratory studies, octopuses have demonstrated that they have good memories and can solve problems. During one experiment, an octopus figured out how to remove a cork from a jar to reach the lobster inside. The next time it was given the jar it opened it much more quickly.

A common octopus is eating a rock crab.

Octopuses learn not only from experience, but also from each other. An octopus can perform a task after watching another octopus do it. This kind of mimicking is usually seen in the most intelligent mammals, such as dolphins. Since an octopus's mother dies before it is born, perhaps that is how it survives—by copying the behavior of other octopuses.

In the ocean, the crafty octopus quickly discovers how to remove tasty fish and crabs from fishermen's traps. When caught in a net itself, it can often make a quick escape. Since it has no bones, an octopus can squeeze its entire body through any hole that is large enough for its small beak to fit through.

At the Seattle Aquarium, a 40-pound (18-kg) giant Pacific octopus once pushed a 66-pound (30-kg) rock lid off its tank and oozed to the floor. Another octopus took every opportunity to squirt water

Scientists are constantly learning more about coleoids.

at the same biologist each time she passed its tank. The biologist used to shine her flashlight into its tank to check the water flow, so perhaps the blast of water was the octopus's way of saying that it didn't care for the nightlight.

Coleoids have excellent eyesight. While humans focus by changing the shape of the lens, coleoids move the whole lens forward and backward, the way you would focus a camera. Most coleoids can turn their eyes 180° to see behind them. Scientists believe coleoids do not see in color, but rather contrast light and dark tones.

Octopuses, squids, and cuttlefish spend most of their lives alone. They may hide in the safety of a den or blend into the ocean habitat until it is time to mate and die.

Scientists long to ask these clever, colorful coleoids many questions. What do the different colors mean? How do you see your world? How do you see us? For now, octopuses, squids, and cuttlefish still carry many of their secrets with them to the lowest depths of the oceans and to the farthest corners of the world.

Words to Know

bioluminescent—the creation of light by chemical reactions in the skin of some animals

Cephalopoda—a class of sea creatures belonging to the Mollusca phylum that share certain traits. Cephalopods have a beak, a head, a mantle, arms, and, in squids and cuttlefishes, two tentacles. Some, like the nautilus, have hard, outer shells.

camouflage—the blending of an animal into its surroundings by changing color, shape, or texture

chemoreceptors—sensory organs located on the undersides of the suckers of coleoids that can touch, smell, and taste

chitin—a hard compound that forms the hard beaks of coleoids and the internal skeletons of squids, and some octopuses

chromatophores—special skin pigmentation cells that a coleoid can contract or expand to lighten, darken, or change color

cirri—thin sensory organs found on the bottom of the arms of some octopuses, such as the deep-sea dumbo octopus

Coleoidea—a subclass of the cephalopod class that is made up of sea creatures, which may or may not have remnants of shells. Octopuses, squids, and cuttlefish are three orders in the subclass Coleoidea.

cuttlebone—the calcium carbonate skeleton of a cuttlefish

den—the home of an octopus; it can be a cave, a pile of rocks, under ledges, or even a soda bottle

invertebrate—animal that does not have a backbone. Ninety-five percent of all marine animals are invertebrates.

ligula—the spoon-shaped tip of a male octopus's arm that is used to transfer a sperm packet to the female

mantle—the muscular, saclike body that encases a coleoid's heart, gills, and other organs

mollusk—the phyla of soft-bodied, invertebrate animals that have external shells, reduced internal shells, or no shells at all

order—animals within a subclass that share certain characteristics. Octopuses make up the order Octopoda, squids belong to Teuthoidea, and cuttlefish are part of the Sepioidea.

pen—the bladelike skeleton of a squid that is made from chitin

photophores—light-producing organs under the skin that allow an animal to become bioluminescent, or lit from within

prey—an animal that is caught and killed by another animal for food

predator—an animal that hunts another animal for food

radula—the sawlike tongue of a mollusk that is covered with tiny, sharp teeth

spermatophore—the packet of sperm that the male coleoid transfers to the female during mating

siphon—a funnel-like opening on a coleoid that is used in breathing, releasing ink, and for jet-propelled swimming

subclass—a group of animals within a class that share certain characteristics. Octopuses, squids, and cuttlefish make up the subclass Coleoidea.

Learning More

Books

Cerullo, Mary M. *The Octopus: Phantoms of the Sea*. New York: Cobblehill Books, 1997.

Llamas, Andreu. *Secrets of the Animal World: Octopuses, Underwater Jet Propulsion*. Milwaukee, WI: Gareth Stevens Publishing, 1996.

Martin, James. *Tentacles: The Amazing World of Octopus, Squid, and Their Relatives*. New York: Crown Publishers, 1993.

MacQuitty, Miranda. *Ocean*. New York: Dorling Kindersley, 1995.

Web Sites & Places to Visit

Monterey Bay Aquarium
886 Cannery Row
Monterey, CA 93940
http://www.mbayaq.org
Explore the habitats of the sea to learn more about cephalopods.

Public Broadcasting Service
1320 Braddock Place
Alexandria, VA 22314
http://www.pbs.org
PBS documentaries explore the giant squid and the vampire squid.

Seattle Aquarium
1483 Alaskan Way
Seattle, WA 98101
http://www.seattleaquarium.org
Learn about cephalopods and other sea animals.

Index

About the Author

Trudi Strain Trueit is a writer and broadcast journalist whose fascination with the undersea world began during childhood trips to the ocean and to the Seattle Aquarium. An award-winning television news reporter for KREM TV (Spokane, WA), she has contributed stories to ABC News, CBS News, and CNN. Ms. Trueit is the author of four weather books in Scholastic's Franklin Watts Library Series: *Clouds*, *Storm Chasers*, *The Water Cycle*, and *Rain, Hail, and Snow*. Ms. Trueit makes her home in Everett, WA, and still visits the ocean and the aquarium whenever she can.